Uh, Maybe Don't?

A Misanthrope's Guide To Not Killing Yourself

Jesse Bosley

Disclaimer

I (the author) am not a trained anything; not a psychologist, psychiatrist, doctor, social worker, airplane pilot, forklift operator, etc. With that said, nothing in this book is professional advice. Everything I say or suggest in this book is strictly my own opinion or experience. You (the reader) take responsibility and claim any and all risk for your own interpretations and actions.

This book does not replace the advice of a medical professional. Consult your doctor(s) before making any changes to your health plan.

If you are in an active state of crisis then please put this book down and call the appropriate services (988 in the US at time of writing).

There's no shame in asking for help; not only are there people who are trained to help you, they WANT to help you. So let them. And when you're feeling better, or at least less shitty, come back and hang out. I'm not going anywhere, this is a book.

ISBN: 979-8-218-36543-1

Contents

An Introduction of Sorts
Who Am I? What Is This?

Hi I'm Jesse,

First off, thanks for buying my book! I'm gonna guess that you picked this up cause the title caught your eye and now you're wondering who the borderline illiterate weirdo writing this is. Especially after the disclaimer made it very clear that I am woefully unqualified to be writing a book, let alone one about such a sensitive subject. Well I'm Jesse…that's all goodnight!

But for real, I'm someone who has dealt with untreated major depression and other mental illnesses for over 20 years and on multiple occasions tried to unsubscribe from life. Despite that, I've always been the person people seek out when they need someone to talk to. It seems all the help I couldn't give myself, I gave to others.

I'm beyond happy to say that there are over a dozen people alive today because of me and my words. And it is my biggest hope that this book boosts that number considerably. I could definitely use the karma. I can't say what exactly about me drew people in and allowed them to absorb what I had to say. Maybe it was my humor, my self-deprecating demeanor, or my hobo-like appearance; I haven't got a clue. But I do know one thing; most people just need a friend and a place to be honest. And that, my friends, is what this book is—or at least what I want it to be.

I want you to think of this book like a really lopsided conversation with a friend. If you've got no one else in your life that you can talk to or share your honest thoughts with, you've got me now. Put me in your bag or pocket or backpack and carry me wherever you go, I'm your companion. Write in my margins, express your thoughts, and fill the pages with your uniqueness. Read me cover to cover or swing by your favorite passage for a visit when you need to. I'll try to show you how to stick around; and along the way, through stories and stray thoughts, you'll get to know me pretty well.

I'm not some self help guru or celebrity, writing from a mansion funded by your tears and fears. I'm not talking down to you as if you're a moron and I'm some 5th dimensional big brain pillar of proper functioning. I'm writing this in my underwear in a one bedroom apartment. I curse too much, have a limited vocabulary, and I make too many movie references. I'm just a human, no better or worse than you, so let's be friends.

With that said, I am a self proclaimed misanthrope. For the longest time I had never heard the word and then one day BOOM! I got a new description for my general world view. If you're unfamiliar like I was about what a misanthrope is, basically they're someone who doesn't like people and avoids society.

Uh, Maybe Don't?

How do you become a misanthrope?

Well for me, I've seen one too many man-made horrors to like humans across the board and society never felt particularly inviting. When life feels like a series of down notes—you tend to become a downer.

So why write a book trying to help people?

The short answer is—I didn't.

The long answer is that while I have a general disdain for the human population; that is mainly because I believe in human potential and have felt betrayed by what modern society did to it. Humans are existences meant to work together and when we do we achieve great things. But this usually only happens at small scale. When humans get in big groups bad things tend to happen, like war. So I curse the big scale and praise the small. In other words—I hate people but I like persons.

Society can eat my whole ass but any individual can shake my hand. So I didn't write this book to help people, I wrote it to help the persons like me. And maybe if those persons see a misanthrope as fucked and jaded as me learn to be happy and want to stick around; they'll realize they can get there too.

So if this is a guide when do I get a map or checklist?

Despite the title, this isn't going to be a standard guide made to be treated as a checklist. This book is basically the book that would have helped me when I needed it most. An honest and humorous first hand account to make me feel like I'm not alone. As cliche as it sounds, this book is meant to be a journey we take together. I'll essentially act as a local tour guide pointing out all the places that

I found special and the stories that made it that way. So hopefully at the end of this you'll have an idea of where you want to go next and some movies/shows you can watch along the way.

With all of that in mind, consider me Samwise Gamgee and yourself Frodo with the ring. I can't carry your suffering for you, but I can carry you to where you need to go.

The Original Fuck Up
Not Planning To Be Here Very Long

"What do you want to be when you grow up?" is a question I never had an answer to; because I never planned to grow up. The chapter title might be a little harsh but it's important to acknowledge how we got here and what it's done to us. I think the first and possibly biggest mistake we make when thinking of suicide, is that it's the end. Now greater minds than me can go around in circles and debate the morality of killing yourself, that's not for me to decide for you. But what I will insist to you, is that thinking of suicide as an end will cause a spiral that poisons your mind and traps you.

<u>What the fuck are you talking about?</u>

Well to me it's simple really, if you view suicide as an end; then it will quickly begin to look like an escape. I am incredibly guilty of using this as a coping mechanism. No matter what was going on in my life; be it bad grades, losing people, rejection, fear of failure, or just fear of the future—I always had suicide in my back pocket.

I honestly thought this was a great strategy for getting through a troubled life. Every challenge or difficulty that I was scared to face was met with me saying *"well if this doesn't work out I can always kill myself."* That ideology was so ingrained in me and I would repeat it so often; that my friends and family would use it to convince me to do GOOD things for myself that I didn't want to do. But that thought is a dangerous crutch.

There's actually a Netflix series called After Life that centers around this idea. In the show the main character even refers to it as a superpower. He believes he can act on whatever impulses he wants and if it goes wrong…well lights out. Now I don't want to spoil the show for you, it's honestly a good watch; but eventually the main character realizes that the same logic can apply to his good impulses. That if you do every good thing you want to do, that you may have been too scared to do before, you might just end up with a life you want to live. That message is why I feel comfortable calling this ideology a crutch.

It seems in the modern lexicon that the word crutch refers to something negative you're overly reliant on and is thus holding you back. That's dog shit and I fucking hate it. A crutch is something you need when you're hurt, it's an important tool in your recovery. Sure, if you always lean on it your injured parts won't regain their strength. But if you don't have something to lean on you'll fall, hurt yourself more, and be unable to move at all. A crutch is not inherently a bad thing, but using it can't be your only effort.

I believe that seeing suicide as an end is the ultimate crutch. It is the last branch you can grab onto as you plummet into the pit of despair and it is terrifying to ever think of letting it go. As long as you hold onto that branch you're safe from the world because nothing can truly hurt you—but you'll never get out of the pit that

6

way. If thinking that way is the only thing getting you moving at all or stopping you from killing yourself right now, then lean on that crutch.

Lean on it and use it to get somewhere better, somewhere safer.

Now I do feel compelled to explicitly state that you shouldn't use this thinking to hurt people or be destructive. The way you use this crutch properly is like the guy in the show. If with this thinking the stakes are zero, then shoot for the damn stars. Is there someone you wanted to try talking to? Start a conversation. If it doesn't work out, who cares? Definitely not you right now. A hobby you've always been interested in but hesitant to start? Better start now, you might be dead soon! And on and on and on. As hard as it may be to believe right now, one of those good things is eventually going to work out.

That's not me being an optimist by the way, that's just statistics. There's an old saying you've probably heard that states: "*If you put a bunch of monkeys in a room with typewriters, given an infinite amount of time, they will eventually recreate all the works of Shakespeare.*" It's crazy to think about but it's true. And you might say that infinity is a powerful thing that you don't have, that's also true. But infinity wouldn't mean shit if those monkeys didn't go in the room. That's what you need to do—go in the room. Put yourself in the position for something to go right and eventually it will.

Big talk from a guy hiding behind a book.

Alright, you want an example? How about the way I got my partner? It's a fun little story that ironically enough involves me literally walking into a room.

At the time we were in college and had only just met. I had a mild concussion from crashing my Razor scooter (Vladimir Scootin') a few days prior on Halloween. I was really depressed and hopeless and just didn't care what happened to me anymore.

So many things had been disappointing and life seemed like such a bother that I didn't want to continue it anymore. But I dragged myself to where our friends were playing drinking games, hoping for one last good night. With the stakes of the evening all of a sudden becoming zero—I decided to be my boldest self. I laughed a little louder, made more jokes, and told more stories. I was enjoying myself and as youthful parties usually went at the time, we eventually found ourselves playing truth or dare.

Now I'm a little bitch 90% of the time, but this night (with the guidance of alcohol) landed in that little 10% sliver. So when the ladies of the room were asked who the most attractive guy was in the room, I took a chance. The only guys there were me and my friend, but I really needed a win. So I told the ladies to hold their judgment as I left the room. A minute or so later I came back, knocked on the door, and said *"Did someone call for an awkward entrance?"* A very cringe thing to say—there was a reason I was alone. But what came next was an even cringier action as I threw open the door and walked into the room wearing nothing but pull away gold stripper shorts.

I had the shorts because I was into Rocky Horror at the time and wanted to go to a screening in costume. They eventually became my ace in the hole during strip poker games, but that's a story for another time. The reaction from the room was definitely mixed but I did manage to peak the interest of my partner who until then thought I was just a cocky asshole. As the night calmed down (I won the vote btw) me and my partner started talking and found we had a lot of common interests. Slowly her view of me turned from a cocky asshole to a confident but awkward person. I offered to show her my favorite movie that night and we've been together for ten years now.

So yeah, I literally took a chance by walking into a room and it was the best decision I ever made. And while I don't want to go too far into romantic relationships (maybe in another book), having a good partner enabled me to better myself and find even more opportunities. Having just one thing go right can change the path you're on, but that won't happen if you don't go into the room.

I wasted so much of my time assuming things were bound to be terrible. Assuming that I would inevitably kill myself, so there was no point in struggling to do better. What was the point of improving myself if I was just going to fail and throw it all away in the end anyway? Thinking that way didn't help me, it just perpetuated the problems I had that made me feel that way in the first place.

If, like me, you spend a lot of your time struggling to see the point in working towards something doomed to fail, here it is. The point is that in working and struggling to improve, you inevitably create more options for yourself. Sure they aren't all going to be tickets to immediate success or perfect solutions to all your problems. But just like the monkeys, the more chances you have available, the more likely you are to stumble into something amazing. Just make sure you remember to pack your shorts.

The opposite outcome is just as true. If you don't plan to stick around very long because life just isn't worth sticking around for, then when the future inevitably arrives—you won't have a plan to deal with it. If you spent all your time thinking you had this one perfect answer to any problem in the form of suicide, you will inevitably fail to develop any alternatives. And without any alternatives you'll be stuck in the same path you've always hated. This almost always leads to life getting worse and worse, making you feel your initial assumptions were correct in some fucked up self fulfilling prophecy.

You need to give yourself more opportunities so you can develop alternative solutions for life's problems. The more options at your disposal, the more likely you are to obtain something good in your life. Once you have something good, that's when you drop the crutch. Sure, before you could always take yourself out and thus you had nothing to lose, well now you do. So you better hang on to it with both hands. No more last branch.

As long as you keep thinking of suicide as an exit you're waiting to take; you'll miss out on all the beautiful things that make staying on the road worthwhile.

That is our original fatal fuck up.

You're Not Crazy
The World Really Is Fucked

Have you noticed that in the past few years there has been a massive uptick in mental health issues? Maybe you're one of the people who feels like your world flipped over night. Like you were moving through life normally, some struggles here and there; but all of a sudden you feel trapped under the weight of yourself?

Yeah, it's not just you and it's not your fault.

Over the past few years the world has lost its damn mind. Crazy politicians, wars, natural disasters; that guy who tailgated you on the highway for like 10 miles flashing his high beams that rival the sun (seriously wtf dude? Just go around). We are living in truly insane times and being affected by that is a normal response. The people who can walk around as if everything in the world is fine right now and continue to go about their normal lives, they're the weird ones. It isn't normal to sit in a burning house and act like it's any other day.

This trend is probably the thing that has gotten under my skin the most. For years, anytime my misanthrope outlook was brought up,

I'd be told that I view the world negatively because I'm depressed. And while depression can definitely cause you to view everything through shit-colored glasses, shit is still going to look and smell like shit. By that I mean that if the world is actually terrible, it's not crazy to view it that way.

So my response to this criticism was always:

> *"I don't think the world is shit because I'm depressed; I'm depressed because the world is shit."*

We as humans are inherently social creatures, it's literally the core source of our survival as a species. We aren't that strong or fast and we don't have natural weapons. Our special power was coming together as a group to get stronger and solve problems.

Ok? What does that have to do with how I'm feeling?

Probably more than you realize. If humans are such social creatures then it makes sense that we developed the ability to sense when something was off with each other. Most of human communication is non-verbal. It's how you read a room, change your manners, and blend in. Anyone who has masked before understands this even if it's subconsciously. In short, humans know how to catch a vibe as a survival instinct.

Do you want to take a guess at what the vibe of the planet has been lately? Yeah, it's not great. Damn near everything has caused our vibe instincts to go into overdrive. Even if you're not actively thinking about it, the state of the world sits in the back of your head.

Personally, anytime I sort the recycling and take it an extra block to the right dumpster to help the environment. Only to see some company take a toxic shit into a river. Or skip out on buying a new game so I can put money into savings for a future that won't come and a house I'll never be able to afford. There's a little voice in the back of my head that's like *"Why bother? What's the point? This will all be pointless soon."*

What makes all of this worse are the people who actively choose to pretend everything is completely fine. For some reason society has told us that when we're out in public we're supposed to lie to each other and pretend to be different people than we are. So when you go outside and all of your instincts are screaming at you that something is wrong; but you look around and everyone is acting normal, it makes you feel crazy. Feeling different from those around you will cause your old lizard brain to think the group has rejected you. Then you end up feeling isolated and all the negative emotions just keep compounding.

<u>So what are we supposed to do?</u>

Well first off realize that when you look online or outside at other people, all you're seeing is a performance. Think of it like going to see a play in the theater. If you were watching a play, would you feel bad for not behaving like the actors? Of course not, that'd be obnoxious as hell. Instead you should observe the people who aren't acting. In this example that'd be your fellow audience members. Understand that the majority of the people in the theater aren't acting on stage. Everyone else is just hard to see because of the direction of the lights. I think this metaphor has gotten away from me.

The point is this, if you're trying to compare yourself to people in public; you'll always lose because you're not playing the same game. In the modern day this issue is multiplied even more by the prevalence of social media. As one of the people who was around at the dawn of social media, I like it. So I'm not gonna completely shit on it. However, anytime researchers look at the effects it has on our brains, what they find isn't good. Even the people who invented the tech behind social media, regret making it.

<u>You're starting to sound old as fuck.</u>

Well I am. You know why? Cause I didn't kill myself! Now shut up and listen. Our brains aren't ready to handle social media in the modern world. Our socially wired little brains love to feel connected and memes are the best part of my day; but the whiplash while scrolling is crazy. I'll go from a news headline about some atrocity and how we're all doomed—to seeing an old acquaintance having a kid and buying a house. This makes me feel like a failure and like I'm the only one seeing the world for what it currently is.

This is all a really long winded way to say; if you feel like you're going crazy right now, you're not. You are having the appropriate emotional reaction to the world you find yourself in. And if you think you're the only one feeling this way, you aren't. Social etiquette just insists we put up a fake glamorized appearance when in front of others. Both on and offline. And the people you see who look like they have it all together are most likely just acting like they do. No one knows the right way to go through life because there isn't one. We're all just faking it. So don't compare yourself to false idols.

Now please realize this isn't a pass to just give up and say fuck it. Instead we should acknowledge the situation so we know how to navigate it and get to the good stuff while mitigating the bad as much as we can. Things are never going to be perfect; not the world, the people in it, and not you either. To expect anything different is only going to cause you pain. And while we may be living in one of the shittier times in history, there is still plenty of fun to squeeze out of this burning blueberry we call Earth. After-all, history shows that the bad times don't last forever.

Even if it doesn't feel that way right now.

Find A Reason To Stay
Value Is In The Eye Of The Beholder

I think it's fair to say that finding the meaning in life is the greatest challenge our species has been trying to solve since we left the caves. Prior to that the only thing that mattered was eat, fuck, sleep, repeat. Maybe some value and attention was put on finding a really cool stick (which we still haven't fully grown out of). But for the most part our lives were consumed by making sure they kept going. All of the skills and abilities we are born with as humans are designed for those kinds of tasks. So what would happen if we weren't in that environment anymore?

In my opinion that question has gone under-explored for far too long. Thanks to society meeting most of our basic needs and shielding us from nature, our natural skill set goes to waste. You don't need to have an adrenaline rush and fight for your life just to get your next meal anymore (unless you're the youngest sibling). So what is your body supposed to do with that reaction in the modern day? Well it ends up manifesting in often inconvenient ways like anxiety.

The feeling of a life or death problem used to be very fast, cause you either lived or died. But in the modern day our problems like failing tests, getting a report in, or making rent cause the same response. Our heart rate goes up—making us anxious, our hunger is suppressed—so we forget to eat, and our minds start to notice every detail around us—making us overstimulated so we start to shut down and get angry.

This reaction was meant to give us the energy and focus we needed to overcome immediate obstacles. The problem is that we can usually see modern problems way before they happen and before we can do anything about them. I once saw a post online talking about this and equating it to being chased by very slow tigers. We know they're chasing us; but they're just out of reach so we can't attack and if we relax for even a moment they'll kill us. So how does our scumbag body respond? Panic, absolute unregulated panic.

Why bring this up? You're not a scientist. Stop embarrassing yourself.

I'm willing to risk embarrassing myself to make this point. Humans, at the end of the day, are animals and we're not in the environment we were designed for. Like a hippo at the ballet or me in the workforce. All of the advantages we're supposed to have are now usually working against us. Humans developed way too quickly for nature to keep up with and that includes our own bodies. We still haven't adjusted to the new world we find ourselves in and that makes it easy to get lost.

People need something to look towards to let them know they're on the right path. In our original environment, it was food and safety. Did your actions allow you to eat AND live? YES?! Then you must be doing something right. It seems modern society's replacement for this guidepost is money. Are your efforts making a profit? Are you making enough money to be useful to others?

How many people do you have more than? This kind of focus is overwhelmingly commonplace. And while I could get into all the historical and political reasons on how that came to be, I've got a more important point to make. You get to choose what you want to value.

The money centric value system simply doesn't work for everyone. And while you unfortunately will have to find a way to coexist with it while in society, you don't have to adhere to it. You may have seen or heard this exchange over the last couple of years:

"What's your dream job?"

"I don't have one, I do not dream of labor."

This is an example of choosing your own guiding value. For some, the society standard of building a career and amassing wealth is all they need and desire out of life. But other people might have a different goal in mind or not have a clear goal at all; and it's important to know that that's okay. When I was younger I heard someone say:

"I really wish I could see what the world would be like if everyone did what they wanted to do before someone told them they'd have to earn a living one day."

Regrettably I was never able to find the source of those words but they've stuck with me. The money centric value system was put into our minds as an absolute fact so early on that we think there aren't any alternatives. And questioning it is usually met with:

"That's just how the world works, that's just life."

And if you're anything like me you might have thought to yourself *"if that's all life is, then I don't want it."* For me that goal wasn't worth sticking around for, the juice wasn't worth the squeeze. I hated myself for not sharing that common goal—it just never felt like it fit me. And of course it didn't; because that goal, that reason for staying, was someone else's. I had been given a single, non-enticing option, and was told it was the only one. So I struggled with justifying staying here for what essentially felt worthless. It felt like I was missing the anchor needed to hold me to this world. But here's the secret I found; anything can be an anchor if it holds enough weight FOR YOU.

If you're like me and find it hard to stay alive just for the sake of staying alive and making money; then you need to find a different reason to stay. With no goal to reach or anchor to keep you tied to this world, humans tend to just wither away. People will often talk about finding their purpose in life. By that they usually mean something they need to do everyday until they die and is thus their reason to wake up and keep staying here. Oftentimes this purpose ends up being some form of job or labor. This view equates purpose to a reason to stay. It implies that you need to be fulfilling a purpose or offering something in order to justify staying alive. This my friend, is a load of shit. The implication that you need to justify your right to exist on any level, is wrong.

You really take a weird path to making a point don't you?

Not always but this point is very close to my heart so I wanted to share my full thought process on it. One of the things I struggle with on a daily basis is feeling like I have to justify the fact that I'm still alive. Due to my mental illness I haven't been able to produce anything, hold a job, or have anything tangible to offer people. I can't exist in the world the way the world wants me to and that means I should leave.

That thought consumes me even now.

Maybe it's because I grew up in the United States, but the only value the world around me seemed to care about was money. And since I had no ability to provide it, I myself must have no value. It took far too long to realize this wasn't true and I still have a hard time reminding myself of that. What started to get me out of that thinking was noticing when it began.

When I was in college I didn't think highly of myself but I didn't think I was completely worthless. Why was that? What I realized was that in that setting the value system was different. When you're in school (high school, trade school, college) everyone is relatively on the same page financially. It is expected that a student is broke or at least not financially independent. Since everyone effectively has the same amount of financial value, it becomes worthless. What usually takes its place is social value. There is a much bigger emphasis placed on who you are rather than what you have—and in that system I had value.

I wouldn't go so far as to say I was popular; but I had a decent number of friends and I could see why they would be friends with me. Not to toot my own horn here but in my college days I was an intelligent, funny, and empathetic guy. Sure, my personality was an acquired taste to say the least; but for my friends I had a lot to offer. I could help with understanding coursework, make them laugh, or just offer a safe place to be vulnerable. I prided myself on the value of these traits and practices—then one day it was gone.

The more I thought about this the more I realized that all of those things about me were still true. Sure I had changed after college, mainly in an effort to adapt to the new world I found myself in. But at my core I was still the same person. I still loved showing people movies they hadn't seen, having deep conversations late into the night, and helping my friends when they were feeling down. All of the things I considered to be good about myself hadn't changed. So why did I feel like a worthless pile of shit with nothing to offer?

Eventually I would have to laugh at the cruel irony of my situation. There was so much I was good at, so much I had to offer. Except for the one thing that mattered. In what can only be called a dick move by life; I had the misfortune of being alive when the only thing that mattered was the one thing I was biologically incapable of. Providing economic value. Fuck me right?

<u>Well at least you figured it out, right?</u>

Sure, but when I figured this out I would constantly bounce back and forth between being ecstatic and wallowing in despair. On one hand I finally had a defense for when my value was questioned; but on the other hand my problem seemed further set in stone. It's not like I could pay my rent with good vibes and movie suggestions. Unless I wanted to escape to the woods, I would eventually need money (straight up that's why I wrote this book, student loans ain't cheap, so thank you).

When I said you would have to learn to coexist with society's money focused value system, this is what I meant. On some level you'll still have to play the game, but you don't need to give yourself the same conditions for winning as everyone else. Winning life is really just about acquiring what is important to you, what you value, and most importantly what makes you happy.

I want you to ask yourself what makes you happy, ask what in the world brings you even the slightest bit of joy. It can be anything— a hobby, a job, an action, a food, a smell, a color, a show, a place, a person. ANYTHING AT ALL! But it's important to remember that you're the one asking the question.

<u>Why is that important?</u>

Because when you ask yourself this question you can do it knowing that the only person who will know your answer is you. You don't have to say something you think you're supposed to say or something that you believe will impress someone. Your answer can be anything; it can be something larger than life or even small and silly. If you feel you need permission to be this selfish, here it is, I give you permission to be selfish when you answer this question. I want you to be selfish when you answer, that would make me happy. So if you can't do it for yourself— then do it for me.

Whatever your answer was, whatever it is in all of existence that makes you feel something positive; that is your reason to stay. It doesn't matter if the world thinks your reason is too small or doesn't count. It's YOUR reason, it only has to have value to YOU. So what if it's weird or silly? It just means you value enjoying life over enduring it.

We get one shot at this life shit, and like it or not the only person we'll have from start to finish is ourselves. So why not make them happy? If the reason you came up with feels very small or short-sighted, I have great news for you. You can change your reason to stay whenever you need and as many times as you want.

Uh, Maybe Don't?

<u>What was your reason?</u>

My reasons started small, I really wanted to have one last good christmas. I'm not religious but I fucking love Christmas. Load me up with some Santa, some cookies, and that Michael Bublé album. I will be in pure warm and fuzzy bliss. So when I felt I didn't want to be here anymore and it was only a month or two before Christmas—making it to Christmas became my reason to stay. Once the holidays were over my reason shifted. Sometimes my reason was just to not make my Mom and Partner sad. Other times it was just because I really want to see how One Piece ends. In fact that was my reason a lot of times. If you haven't watched/read One Piece, start, cause it's good enough to keep a lot of us here.

My fanboying aside, I hope you see that anything big or small can be a valid reason to stay. When you find something that makes you happy and is important to you, try to figure out what about it makes you feel that way. What is so special about this thing that it makes you want to keep living? Once you figure out what that core value for yourself is, it becomes way easier to find more things that have it.

For me the things that I placed value in were laughter, story-telling, comfort, and close connections. So now I know what events or people or things make me want to keep living. Gone are the days of pining over money and hating myself for failing to become rich. Now I just need to coexist with money just enough to get to the things I actually value in this life. The things I consider a worthy reason to stay.

Those of us fortunate/cursed enough to get to make and follow our own value systems, have endless options. Society is still a pretty recent development all things considered and we as a species still haven't figured out what the right goal to make in this environment is. So why not give your version a shot? Whether it's something larger than life or small enough to fit in the palm of your hand. As long as you're happy and satisfied with your life, you'll only have to coexist with current society just enough to achieve your reason for staying. But you gotta have a reason.

Uh, Maybe Don't?

Because without a reason to stay,

you'll only keep finding reasons to go.

Small Pills And Dollar Bills
Maybe It Is In Your Head

Alright so this next bit has traditionally had some negative feelings attached to it, but as your friend I'd like you to hear me out. When it comes to mental health there is a long history of different ways to approach it. And if you ask me, most of that history is absolutely fucked. Like thank God (or Gandalf, whatever G you prefer) I wasn't mentally ill in the 50s and 60s. The "treatment" those people received was nothing short of horrific and a far shot from anything beneficial.

Fortunately we don't live in those times anymore and the science behind mental health treatment is actually treated as a science now. There are researchers and tests and studies and oversight committees. Multiple fields of study exist now in order to find every healthy angle to approach care from. The two most relevant ones for us are going to be psychology and psychiatry. If you've never known a difference between the two it's basically this; psychology = how thoughts work, and psychiatry = how brains work. Again, I'm not a professional, but that's always been the easiest way for me to think about it.

Uh, Maybe Don't?

These fields often work in tandem with one another because life is one big complicated son of a bitch and simple solutions are rarely found. Luckily for us, society decided upon division of labor millennia ago. This means we can go about our lives while someone more equipped can look into the complicated inner workings of the human mind.

We need to think of mental health the same way we do physical health. Both will have a major impact on your life and both usually have modern treatment options available. But years of stigma and bad experiences have made many forsake the medical approach. I am guilty of doing this.

So why try to convince me?

For twenty years I refused to acknowledge the need for a medical approach to my problems. I was convinced that I could just out think my illness, that I was so intelligent I could will myself through this. I even continued to think that way after trying to kill myself multiple times. Like clearly toughing it out wasn't working but I was convinced these attempts were just a fluke or a temporary failing in my practice. That was so incredibly dumb and narcissistic that I want to hide that truth away forever; but we're friends here, and friends don't lie to each other.

I spent so much time, like SO MUCH TIME, going through intro- spection and trying to figure myself out. Trying to get to the core of who and what I was. If I had to estimate it, I probably would spend somewhere between three to eight hours a day just diving into my own mind. I questioned what I really thought about things, be it a movie or social issues in the world; and then I'd question why I thought the way I did. I would rehearse conversa- tions that hadn't happened yet to make sure I could express myself properly if the topic in question ever came up. I picked myself apart and turned over every side of me, all the while telling myself THIS was the healthy approach. I thought that because I did this it meant I knew myself fully; that a therapist would have nothing left to find so there was no point in going to see one. The work they would do was already done.

I thought this made me better than regular people, and admittedly I still kind of do. What can I say, it's hard to change overnight. Just because I'm writing this book doesn't mean I'm cured. If you think that disqualifies me from speaking on all of this, then so be it. But I think some of the best help often comes from people who share the same experiences as you. I'll go on to talk about the benefits of professionals, but I believe you can't see the entirety of an issue if you only ever see it from the outside. So this whole book is just me standing shoulder to shoulder with you and trying to get us out of this mess from the inside out. I hope you'll accept me taking the lead on this one. Thank you.

So I did all that thinking and for what? Whole nights, hell whole YEARS, wasted stuck in my own head—missing out on every-thing around me. And while I did end up understanding myself and how I work, it didn't make me any better. My mind was a runaway train and even though I could see the problems coming miles down the track; I couldn't get off. I could know exactly what I had to do to get better, how to do it, and I would want to do it—but I just couldn't. There was some kind of block in my head that no amount of mental fortitude or breathing techniques or walks through nature could fix. There was a literal physical issue preventing me from implementing the knowledge I got from all that introspection.

Years of spiraling like this, being unable to hold a job or maintain friendships, or just be a functioning member of society, had turned me into a shell of my former self—cannibalized from the inside. Oftentimes I still feel that I am.

If any of what I just described was relatable to you, please listen close. The thing I needed, that I'm sure anyone who has received professional help before has been screaming at the page, was medication. If that word pushes you away just hold me at arms length and listen to what I have to say.

You see, the brain is basically a big control room for your body. It looks at what's happening, reads reports from the other organs, and directs resources where they need to go. Oftentimes those resources are chemicals that dictate how we feel or how our body develops. However, the human brain is an organ—a super fucking complicated organ, but an organ like any other. As such it can get sick or be malformed. That's just part of being a living organism. It's all up to random chance and it's no one's fault (well maybe one of the G's [God, Gandalf, Gaia] if you're into that sort of thing, but I digress). So what happens if your brain is sick or built a little different? Well this is where all that science I talked about earlier starts to come in.

The control room can fuck up in any number of ways. The control operator might be drunk at the wheel, some of the reports get lost in the mail, and sometimes they just don't have the chemicals they need in stock. Now psychiatrists have spent a ton of time and money watching this little control room like some kind of outside supervisor from corporate. After observing it for so long they've got a good idea on how most of the common problems can be solved. These solutions take the form of medication. Sometimes the medication restocks the chemicals, sometimes it fixes the mail slot and collects reports, and sometimes it takes the bottle out of the control operator's hand.

As far as my non-doctor knowledge goes, that's what mental medication does. It's not always perfect and sometimes when you fix one issue it causes another to pop up. But it tries to fix problems that we can't control ourselves and there shouldn't be any shame in that. You wouldn't think you were a useless piece of shit because you took an Advil for a headache would you? It's the same thing with mental meds.

So I just need the magic pill?

Medication isn't exactly a one-size-fits-all type of deal. You and a licensed psychiatrist are going to have to find what dosage or combination of medications works for you, and that can take awhile. But for me it's what I needed. I could spend all the time and effort in the world trying to force myself to be better. But if I can't get into the control room of my brain, it'd all be meaningless. I still have a ways to go before I'm where I want to be and medication can't take me there; but it cut the chains I couldn't reach and allowed me to start moving forward.

Damn, things got a little heavy there for a minute, sorry about that. Let's change things up. Have you ever seen Good Will Hunting? Fantastic movie, honestly it's my favorite, I could watch it everyday; but I don't want to cheapen the experience. If you're unfamiliar with the movie, it's a film from 1997 that I found way too relatable. It was written by and stars Matt Damon and Ben Affleck, it's the movie that really put them on the map. Which to me is crazy to think about considering they wrote it when they were in their mid twenties and it won a fucking Oscar for best writting. But that's all technical stuff that doesn't really matter here; sorry, my film degree gets the best of me sometimes. I bring up the movie because it created a standard in my mind when it comes to therapy.

Uh, Maybe Don't?

To bring you up to speed; the movie follows the titular main character Will Hunting who is by all appearances a regular guy. He works low end jobs, drives around with his friends, and gets into fights from time to time. He's someone that those in higher society would look at and think he's just another bum from the south side of Boston. But here's the thing, Will is actually a genius. The kind of genius you only see in movies where he can pretty much figure out anything he studies. He clearly has the potential to go as far as he wants in life, so why is he here? That's the question the movie spends its runtime figuring out when circumstances land Will in court ordered therapy. There's a lot more to the movie and some of the best lines you'll ever hear so go watch it. But it's his time in therapy and his relationship with his therapist that I want to focus on.

The therapist who Will ends up seeing is Sean, played by Robin Williams with an Oscar winning performance. And ever since I saw this movie I swore the only therapist who could ever help me was one like Sean. He didn't force Will to lay on a couch and answer his questions, he took his time, and formed an actual relationship with him.

In probably the best scene of the movie Sean starts their second session by taking Will (who was combative in the first session) to the park. They sit down and Sean gives my favorite speech from any movie ever. He acknowledges Will and his intelligence as well as his shortcomings. He talks to him like a regular person and showcases the importance between experiencing life through thoughts versus through action. Sean opens up about his life and then leaves the ball in Will's court, giving him the option to choose to engage or not. After this conversation things change between them and their dynamic slowly switches to something more akin to that of friends.

When I tell you I was obsessed with this dynamic, I mean I was OBSESSED. I couldn't figure out why for the longest time. The answer was that their relationship was what I needed so badly in my life. Looking back on it now, it was probably the first true example of a safe space I'd ever seen.

One line of Sean's speech in particular has always stood out to me. He's telling Will that he wants to know who Will is, not just what he knows; and the only way that happens is if Will talks about himself. He follows that saying:

> *"But you don't want to do that, do ya sport? ...You're terrified of what you might say."*

Like DUDE! Just fucking @ me next time. Have you ever seen yourself reflected so clearly in a sentence that you're almost offended? That singular line struck at the core of why I didn't want to go to therapy. I knew something was wrong with me—I mean shit, while I did all that introspection I was bound to stumble across a trauma or two. But for me it was one thing to know my faults and something else entirely to admit them to someone. What if they think I'm a monster? What if they lock me up in grippy sock jail? What if they tell me I was right to hate all these parts of myself?

But here's the hard truth about questions like that. Until I had an answer, I would always be tormented by the question. My anxiety would eat me alive one small part at a time until I got answers. And the more my anxiety ate away at me, the less of myself I had left to fight off my depression. It was a war on two fronts and winter was coming. So I bit the bullet but didn't eat it. I went to find myself a Sean and the process felt like I was storming the beaches of Normandy.

Uh, Maybe Don't?

<u>That was a lot of war metaphors.</u>

Yeah, maybe being mentally ill in a military focused nation for thirty years did some damage, oh well. The gist of it was this: I couldn't get rid of the depression overnight, but I could get the answers to my anxiety with a phone call. It was terrifying and a fight all its own, especially with the American health care system always seeming to work against me. But it was a fight worth taking. This anxiety over how people would respond to my honest self was a weight I carried for so long, I forgot how heavy it actually was. I even wrote a short passage/poem about this years ago that I will shamelessly insert here:

> *"Sometimes I think that I loved puzzles so much that I turned myself into one. And when no one could or wanted to figure me out and piece me together, I got angry and depressed, not realizing how hard I made it to love me. But eventually I found those persistent enough to find my corners and edges. Slowly they worked their way in, until they found that several pieces were missing, purposefully left out of the box. It was only then that I realized my biggest fear and the steps I had taken to avoid it. I wasn't afraid of people not piecing together my puzzle. I was afraid that once they had—they would hate the picture staring back at them."*

So I finally arrived at traditional talk therapy. While it's definitely not for everyone, you'd be surprised at how much it helps just to have someone to listen to you. Now starting therapy is kinda like starting medication. It can take some trial and error to find which therapist clicks with you and how often you need to see them.

If like me you're scared to start or don't believe it'll be helpful, just remember that I felt the same way and am here admitting something I hate for the whole world to see.

I was wrong.

Something that I was incredibly thrilled to find out is just how much talk therapy has changed in the last few years. While you can still find therapists who subscribe to the old school, cold and cut off approach to the practice, there are starting to be more therapists like Sean. Which approach is better is still debated within the psychologist community; but as far as I'm aware the modern approach involves forming a connection and providing help through empathy. Like surprise surprise, people respond better when you treat them like actual living beings instead of a test subject to analyze. Shocker.

<u>I'm still not sure.</u>

Ok, let's talk about what specific benefits talk therapy can provide. I think too often when therapy is brought up, folks just say it helps or makes you better and they never really explain why. Well as I previously said, just having someone or someplace to talk about your life and thoughts freely is SO liberating. Oftentimes those of us with mental illness bottle up our emotions because we're either scared of how people will react to us or we don't want to be a burden to them. So having a place where we're not just allowed to voice our thoughts and feelings; but also encouraged to do so, lifts a massive weight you might not know you're carrying. Like have you ever noticed you feel physically better after a good cry? It's kinda like that but for your brain or soul or whatever.

Depending on your situation, talking through things may uncover issues you've forgotten or repressed. These can be painful to remember—they were for me. But having someone beside you who knows exactly how to help you through that pain is invaluable. And uncovering those memories can offer you a vital clue for the next benefit.

Something that I severely underestimated the value of was getting a diagnosis. Like for me I always thought that if I knew what my bad behaviors/habits were then I could manage them. But those are usually just symptoms of an actual illness that can have hidden traits affecting you that you'd never notice without having a specific term to look into. Like I did so much stuff that I thought was perfectly normal because I had always done it (like rehearsing conversations in advance). Come to find out I was just severely unwell. And once I had names for all these issues it felt like it took some of their power away. No longer are they some threatening stranger lingering in the dark, now they're just my annoying and predictable roommates. Before, depression and anxiety felt like some bodybuilder holding me down with a knife to my throat. Now they feel like Kyle who bitches at me if I open the curtains too early or forget to take out the trash.

Most importantly, getting a diagnosis through therapy will basically give you a map to hand to your psychiatrist, if you need one. Without that map there's a chance you could be looking in the complete wrong direction. This is why most people find that a combination of talk therapy and medication works for them. At the very least both options are worth looking into.

Nowadays everyone seems quick to call any experience a journey, but mental health can be seen as taking a road trip. Therapy helps you to figure out where you need to go and what road blocks you might encounter; and medication puts gas in your car so you can actually get there. This is a heavy oversimplification but it's the easiest way I've found for us regular folks to understand it.

<u>Alright, let's say I want to try it. What now?</u>

What comes next (at least for the USA) is how to actually get the care you need. I've spent my whole life broke so mental health-care never seemed like an actual option to me. Fortunately, mental health is being taken more seriously nowadays and more insurance companies offer some form of coverage. I won't lie to you and say it's cheap, but there are more affordable and accommodating options now. You may have seen ads for online therapy options. These can be great if you struggle with getting out of the house or don't have a convenient means of transportation. They can also be cheaper since the provider doesn't necessarily need to pay for an office, but that's not a given. Even if it is a bit pricey, it's worth it. Hell, money won't mean anything if you're dead.

Personally, I was only able to get help once I hit economic rock bottom after burning out. I was incredibly lucky to live in a state with a great medicaid/government insurance program. Since I had no income I was put in the absolute lowest category and was able to see most doctors and get most treatments/medications completely free of charge. I didn't have a ton of options/doctors to choose from and all medication was generic; but there's no denying I was overwhelmingly lucky to have such access. It gave me a view into what having socialized healthcare could be like and it felt like a dream.

If you think such assistance is wrong, I encourage you to think again. I've gotten pretty personal in this book so I'm not gonna be shy about a single political paragraph. Having a social safety net allowed me to recover from something I never could on my own. For a year or two of care I can now offer decades of help to society, including this book. Basically the cost to benefit ratio for society is incredibly lopsided in society's favor. There's also the whole empathy side to this and the fact that the whole point of society was to help each other in order to achieve our best outcomes. So if you need assistance like I got, I truly hope you get it and don't feel any shame for accepting it.

<u>Anything else?</u>

Yeah, one last thing to cover in this whole medical section is vitamins. It might sound crazy but they actually do play a vital role in your overall health. I honestly always thought vitamin supplements were a scam, but I was wrong once again. When I first started trying to get my mental health in check; I went to see my regular doctor. One of the first steps he had me do was get blood-work done to see what was going on in my body.

Turns out I had practically no Vitamin D or Vitamin B12 in my system. When I first heard this I was like *"whoa letters, what ever will I do without my letters."* Turns out these letters were actually super important for my brain to function properly. Both vitamins do a variety of things but for me it boiled down to this. Vitamin D is one of the things in your body that allows you to feel good and happy. Vitamin B12 is one of the things you need to feel energized.

So I basically found out I had none of the things that my body needed to make me happy or give me energy to work on anything. No fucking surprise I felt like shit and couldn't accomplish even basic tasks. I changed my diet a little bit and now take a daily supplement and I feel closer to being a person again. So don't overlook what a regular doctor visit and some blood work can do for you.

At risk of sounding like a corny children's program, knowledge is power. So go see your doctors, find out what your body is or isn't doing, and make the changes you need.

Have A Bad Day
It's Okay To Fail

If you're reading this book I think it's safe to say that you've had quite a few bad days already. You may even feel that you only have bad days. But that's not the kind of *have* I'm talking about here. I know this one seems a bit odd; but honestly that's the vibe of this whole book—so you should be on board by now.

It might be a bit hard to explain in text but I'm gonna try. So far when you've had a bad day, it may be more appropriate to say a bad day has happened to you. You have been inflicted with a plight of shit in the form of twenty four hours. Every step you take lands you in a pile of dog shit, every word you say is the wrong one, and everyone seems to hate you for doing all this seemingly on purpose. Those kinds of days have filled my calendar year round like clockwork. Bad days like that absolutely positively fucking suck. Worst of all they're like Thanos, or me making a terrible joke—inevitable.

So what DO you mean by HAVE a bad day?

I mean it the same way Greg Davies has a good meal. You can look up "Greg Davies: You Magnificent Beast." It's a stand-up special (a good one) and if you go to about the 4 minute mark you'll see what I'm referencing. Basically, he talks about having less to look forward to in life as he ages. So when he goes for a good meal he fucking HAS it. He indulges in it and takes note of all the little bits coming together to form the complete experience. Just diving into the moment head first.

That is what I want you to do when it feels like you're having a bad day. To be clear I don't mean to do this for the super shitty bad days I described above. Do this on days that just feel like shit but don't have anything particularly remarkable about them. If you feel like you're having a bad day, do your best to just observe it. I know this is gonna be hard, I can't do this on most days. But if you're able to kinda take a step back from your life and think about it in third person, you'll see that you shouldn't take it personally.

Oftentimes when I have a bad day, I get overwhelmed with this feeling of *"Why ME?"* Like which God's coffee did I piss in for them to hate me today? After a while I start to feel that this is just the natural order of the world. I missed the bus? Just my luck. I got a bad grade on a test/fucked up at work? Of course I did, I'm such a fucking moron. And on and on and on. Bad days, as someone mentally ill, feel like dominoes that are just out of reach. Each domino is something bad and as soon as they start I just look for the next one to fall, never even considering that I could stop it. It's so easy to get swept up in the negativity, especially if that's your go to response.

Uh, Maybe Don't?

For this next bit bear with me as I talk on something I'm under educated on. We're getting medical once again—so strap in! Have you ever thought about how your brain physically works? Basically there's a bunch of nodes that are linked together and send electric signals to different parts of the brain in order to trigger specific responses. These links are called your neural pathways. They're like phone lines linking the control rooms in your head together. And in a giant fuck you to our species, our brains will develop favorites over time. You can think about it like auto-complete when you enter a search. Your brain will see the first few letters and skip to fill in the rest.

<u>What's so bad about that?</u>

Well the more frequently you think a certain way, the more your brain will default to it. So if your response to something is negative or pessimistic thoughts, your brain will start to put you in that head space faster and faster. This is one of the things that causes us to spiral. The good news is that we can form new pathways over time and retrain our brain for better responses. This process is super hard and tiring but it's also very worth it.

That's why I'm recommending you to have a bad day. If you feel like a bad day is starting to happen (preferably a mild one), just accept it and observe the events. It can almost feel like an out of body experience or derealization. So if you struggle with that kind of stuff or just don't feel up to it yet—maybe skip this one. But for me I've found it way easier to accept a bad day and not get bothered by it when I stop making myself the main character. When events stop being things that happen TO ME and start being things that JUST HAPPEN, I start to feel better. It's almost like shifting the blame. The day isn't bad because I suck, sometimes days just suck. And if you wanna hear a really deep secret, get in close I don't want others to hear…sometimes the days don't suck, we just think they do.

Let's take ourselves on a journey through an example of having a bad day.

Our alarm goes off, we blindly hit snooze, it goes off again, we check the time.

What the fuck do you mean it's been thirty minutes?!

Ok we're running late but we can still make it, just gotta skip the shower and use extra deodorant. We actually manage to get to work/class a few minutes early and have some time to collect ourselves and say hi to our peers or check our phone. As the day reaches its midpoint slump we notice we're not too tired, I guess those extra thirty minutes were needed.

After having lunch our boss/teacher yells at us for making a mistake on some previous work.

We shrink into ourselves a bit but when we look over we see them yelling at the top performer for a mild mistake. Maybe we didn't mess up too badly, they're just angry today. We wrap up our day, feeling the exhaustion finally catching up with us.

We head home and it's raining, great. In our rush this morning we forgot to check the weather and didn't grab an umbrella, stupid mistake.

But it's been dry lately so rain wasn't to be expected, honest mistake. Plus since we rushed here we're parked closer to the building so we won't even be in the rain that long.

Uh, Maybe Don't?

We get stuck in traffic, same shit everyday, we spent all day on bullshit and we just want to be home, but noooo all these assholes gotta take MY route!

Well, if we think about it, we're just another asshole holding up their commute. Guess this is just part of being in society.

We get home, a little wetter than we'd like, and realize we didn't pull anything out for dinner, fuck.

It's alright, frozen nuggets aren't too bad and at least there won't be any cleanup. The night finally claims us as we're watching our favorite show trying to recoup from the day.

We pass out a little early and forget to take that shower we missed.

But we'll be well rested tomorrow and can grab one before we leave. As our thoughts fade to dreams we think about all the things we messed up today but on second look they really weren't too bad and some weren't even our fault. Oh well, tomorrow is another day. Then you have this badass dream about dragons and being rich and you have a cool sword.

Okay that last line was just for fun, but you see what I mean about having a bad day? That day was completely normal and it would have been so easy to spiral the moment we overslept. But these mundane events aren't that serious and even when they're our fault it isn't the end of the world. Reminding ourselves of that throughout the day and paying attention to how the world operates around us and not just to us; will help make even bad days feel not so bad.

It gets easier overtime as your brain accepts the new pathways and this practice can help make spirals not so steep. It's okay to be upset when bad things happen or frustrated when plans don't work out; but the most important thing is to remember it's okay to fail.

Not everyday is gonna be a banger and no amount of positive self talk, meditation, or jade vag eggs are gonna change that. There seems to be this pushed narrative that we have complete control over our lives and that if anything wrong ever happens it's our fault. We're expected to somehow give 110% everyday, produce perfect work, and act like that's not a mathematical impossibility. But despite whatever these peer pressure motherfuckers say, humans are not machines. It is ridiculous and cruel to suggest that we can function the way a machine does.

As living creatures, our energy naturally fluctuates throughout the day, the week, and even the month. Anyone who's ever had to buy pads knows how true that is. Some days we're gonna be ready to go all out and get everything done; and some days our bed might as well be the entire world. So if you try to rip someone out of a bed day and force them to have a go all out day, you can't be surprised when they fail or eventually break down. Shit even the machines the world seems to idolize require maintenance. Rest is good and failure should be expected.

Failing is an inevitable part of life, everyone on Earth fails. The part that we control is how we react to failing. Beating ourselves up because we didn't live up to this fantasy idea of how a normal society member functions is pointless. When you inevitably fail; acknowledge it, try to figure out what to improve for next time, and move on.

Uh, Maybe Don't?

One of the greatest quotes I've ever seen comes from Star Trek. Well for me it came from a screenshot of Star Trek I saw online— but the value remains the same!

> *"It is possible to commit no mistakes and still lose. That is not a weakness. That is life."*

I honestly don't think I could put it any better so I kind of want to end the chapter here. But since I think this point is so important, let me say it as directly as I can. In case no one has told you before:

It's okay to fail.
You don't have to be perfect.
Perfect doesn't even exist.
<u>Failing doesn't make you a failure.</u>

Everyone has bad days and it's not your fault. But accepting it, and wallowing in it, are different things. Changing how we naturally respond is difficult but not impossible. Start small and allow yourself the time to change. This life shit is pretty long if you let it be—so you got time.

I hope in the future you have a bad day and don't just have it happen to you.

Good Luck.

Have A Good Day
The Stuffy Nose Theory

Turns out that good days are just as inevitable as bad ones, who knew? So when a good day finally comes alon-

<u>Well actually-</u>

Before your depressed ass doubts that and rolls its eyes at me—shut up. When a good day comes along fucking HAVE it. Pay attention to what is happening to make it a good day and savor it. Depressed people often chase good days like dogs chase cars; with no idea what they'll do when they finally get one. It's natural for us to just enjoy a good day since they're so rare. But if you pay attention and recognize the ingredients of a good day—you'll notice they don't have to be rare at all.

I call this the Stuffy Nose Theory. The core of it is that when your nose isn't stuffy and works normally, you don't notice it at all. But the moment you get a stuffy nose; you can't help but think back to when your nose wasn't stuffy and how you took that for granted. Because of that experience I try to remember this at least once a day when my nose is working and revel in that small victory. Similarly, there are probably tons of little things in your daily life that you appreciate but don't take note of. So if you pay attention to your good days when everything is going right, not only will you appreciate it more, but you're likely to notice how simple the things making it good are. A soft smile from a stranger, a good meal, a funny joke, or even just a good nap. Realizing it just takes a few simple things going right to make your entire day; feels like getting new eyes.

This practice really starts to shine on normal days. We talked about lessening a bad day and feeling even better about a good one. But what about standard days? Well once you notice what made your good days good and how to let mildly bad things slide; your regular days get a shit ton better. Sure it's cool to get better at getting through bad days; but it's fucking amazing to have the blueprint to turn a regular day into a good one. It's not a 100% sure thing, once again we are human after all. But I really think this is one of the keys to a happy life.

If you want to see an example of how all this works (or just want to see a good movie) then I insist you watch "About Time." It's a movie close to my heart from 2013. The movie is a rom-com with a fun twist. The main character learns that the men in his family can travel back in time. This time travel just takes them back to an earlier part of their life. So sadly they can't do cool shit like riding dinosaurs. Instead, each of the family members use this ability to pursue different things. And the main character decides he'll use his power for love. The dude basically gets infinite chances to try and make dates go well. Many laughs ensue.

Without spoiling any of the movie's events; by the end of the movie the main character adopts a new mindset. He starts living each day twice. The first time through he lives it normally, enduring all the ups and downs that life can bring. Then on the second go round he tries to take time to notice all the beautiful little things he was too busy to notice before. It's literally the ideal version of what I've spent these two chapters talking about.

<u>What if you don't have fancy time powers?</u>

Then you'll have to follow the main character's final mindset. Instead of repeating every day, he lives each day as if he's chosen that day in particular to revisit. He tries to notice all the good things the first time around and to view every day as special.

As you go through your regular day to day life just keep your eyes open. I found that it initially helped me to write a note in my phone each time something made me feel good. Our brains are tricky little shits that will try to convince us they'll remember something and then immediately toss those memories out when we aren't looking. So by making a little note throughout the day or week, I could actually remember what made me happy. And once I knew the things that made my days better, I could seek them out whenever I needed to.

<u>Like what?</u>

Well for me one of the little things I could do that made my day better was singing in the car. Singing is something I like but I'm embarrassed by it. So doing it privately in the car allows me to comfortably do something I like and in doing so I get to release some bottled emotions. It's something so simple but it really works to flip my mood around. So if I'm having a bad or even just a meh kind of day, I know how to make that day a bit better whenever I want. Other little things for me were watching my favorite shows, writing little poems on my phone, and making someone laugh. It's also important to enjoy things that aren't in your control, like hitting mostly green lights during your commute. Take every little win you can and make your own when you need to.

Finding your own joys and remembering to seek them out to improve your day takes time, it's a skill you need to practice. Just remember that if you fail at first that's perfectly normal. But please don't give up or worse write this practice off and not even try. I used to scoff at anything that sounded even remotely close to this. But once again I am here telling you I was wrong. This shit doesn't make everything better or change your life overnight, but it will help to change YOU so that you can change your life.

I want to be clear that this change isn't a complete rewriting of who you are. There's a common fear amongst us mentally ill folk that if we cure or treat our illness, there won't be any of ourselves left. If you've been unwell for a long time it may be hard to remember being any other way. In a sense we feel that we are our illness, we are all of the things wrong with us. This was one of my biggest fears. I thought that if I messed with my mind and started acting differently, that I'd be losing and betraying my true self. I have been so incredibly ill since I was just seven years old. All of my development and experiences were done as someone sick, it's so closely tied in with my personality at this point. So if I removed the sickness, why wouldn't all of me go with it? If you have had similar thoughts, please know that they are normal—and they are also wrong.

Our illness is not the founding pillar of who we are, without which we crumble. It's more accurate to say that our illness is a glass ceiling on our ability to be ourselves. As I got treatment I didn't feel like someone else. I felt like I got to be the version of myself I previously could only visit on my best days. So don't shy away from change and don't rush it either. Let it happen at its own pace and enjoy being reunited with all the parts of yourself that you missed.

Simplify Your Life (With Help)
Improvise. Adapt. Overcome.

Over the course of my life I've had a few opportunities to be around very successful people. While their personalities and morals left much to be desired, I tried to see what I could learn from them. From the outside these people seemed to live the craziest, most hectic lives possible. I thought there must be something wrong with them. Afterall, you could offer me all the money in the world and I still wouldn't willingly run multiple companies. But the more I learned about them there was one thing I noticed they all did. Every single one of them simplified their lives as much as possible.

<u>What do you mean they simplified their lives? How?</u>

Well it's pretty simple, they outsource everything they possibly can. That sounds pretty typical for rich people but their reasoning for doing this is what makes them a completely different type of people. See, when we think about our day, we try to cram in everything we want or need to do. I'm sure more than once on a busy day you've heard the expression *"There just aren't enough hours in the day.* We'll grumble like that and then try to fit everything we couldn't do today into tomorrow. What else are we gonna do? It's not like you can just create more hours in the day…or can you? While you can't create more hours in the day, you can buy someone else's. After all, we live in a money focused society, everything is for sale! And it just so happens that your average person is already used to being paid by the hour. This bit is gonna get into economics a little, but stick with me—I promise I have a point.

The average day of a working class person is usually broken up into three chunks that are eight hours each. One chunk is for sleeping, one chunk is for their job, and the third chunk is for everything else in their life. For most of us these chunks aren't nearly this balanced but this is how we tend to think about our day. The chunk that usually gets the most attention is the job chunk. This chunk has a tendency to cannibalize the other chunks whenever it needs a little more wiggle room. But since this chunk is what affords us the money we need to live, we're willing to overlook their crimes.

Speaking of money! That's what this is all about. You sell your biggest chunk for some money and your employer is happy to buy it. You then take that money and buy the things you need like food, water, and a big screen TV. If you're anything like me you'll eventually find yourself in the store looking at an item and thinking *"Huh, this is worth an hour of my life."* It can be a pretty upsetting thought but you need to eat so you keep selling the hours. But why is your employer so happy to buy them? That's easy, it's because they know they're getting a good deal.

This is the main point to everything so I'll stop beating around the bush. Rich people know they can get money whenever they want, but they're stuck with the same twenty four hours each of us get in a single day. This makes time the most valuable resource to them and they have to spend it wisely. So if they can use money to get eight hours of your time and thus save eight hours of their own, that's a good deal. It becomes even better for them when it produces more money than it costs. In other words, they pay you less than your worth, profit the difference, and then they still get to keep your eight hours. This is the fundamental system that employment is currently based on.

The biggest gain in this exchange wasn't the money. Sure they just made money for doing essentially nothing; but that's just smoke and mirrors to distract you. The real gain is that while that was happening, they could use the eight hours they saved to work on a different goal they have. That's how they get the most out of their most limited resource—time. And you can do the same thing on a smaller scale.

Like everyone else we only have twenty four hours in a day. But unlike everyone else, those of us with mental illness don't have as much mental energy to use during the day. A common way to express this is by using the example of spoons. You start your day with a drawer containing a random amount of spoons. Each task you do takes a certain amount of spoons based on how difficult that task is for you to deal with. Getting a snack might be a one spoon activity while washing the dishes could be a ten spoon activity. Once you know how many spoons something costs you can more wisely choose how to spend them.

<u>What does this have to do with rich people and the economy?</u>

This is where the practice of outsourcing like the rich comes in. For the same amount of spoons that it takes you to wash the dishes, you could do five other things. So instead of wasting ten spoons on the dishes, find a way to get them done for less spoons. If you have the money you can straight up hire someone to do it for you. You could switch to using paper plates so there aren't as many dishes. You could just put them in the dishwasher while they're completely dirty and run it twice to get everything completely clean. There's a lot of creative ways to lower the spoon cost of many things in your life. Figuring out the best ones is the key to making the most of your day.

What if you don't have money? How do you save spoons when you're broke?

Well allow me to introduce you to support systems!

Having a solid support system is one of the most beneficial things that will improve your life. Humans are social creatures, hell we looked at wolves and thought *"If not friend then why friend shaped?"* Despite what our illness might tell us—we're not meant to be alone. The entirety of society and human advancement only came about because people worked together. It's tempting to want to write off other people as a constant source of disappointment you'd be better without. The less people you confide in and trust, the less people there are to let you down or betray you. Even our media portrays stories of loners as the ultimate cool variant of self reliance.

I bought into this very hard and at times I tried to make myself an unapproachable island of a person. Narcissism and fear played equal parts in me developing this mindset and behavior. I thought that if I became the one person who truly doesn't need anyone else; that would make me special, better than those around me. After years of being called worthless, inside and outside of my own mind, the thought of being verifiably better was alluring. Add in the fear of being let down or made fun of by people I was supposed to trust, or being a burden to those I loved; and isolationism looked better and better everyday. It's a pretty easy thought pattern to spiral into when you have the right combination of illnesses. But just as there are only twenty four hours in a day or a limited number of spoons in the drawer; there were only so many things I could do on my own. And getting better, for me, wasn't one of them.

My intention isn't to sell short the efforts anyone has taken to improve themselves. Change comes from within after all. And sometimes removing people from your life is a positive (more on that later). But self improvement, in the long run, has a glass ceiling.

Okay, so we've established that having help from others is a good and necessary thing for us to get better, great. How the fuck do we actually do that though? What does it look like in the real world? Well the truth is it looks different for everyone and I know that answer sucks ass. Luckily I do think there are some common traits that we can hone in on. Again these are just rough guidelines, adjust them as needed, there will be a bit of trial and error involved in this. But that's fine, because as we've already established, it's okay to fail.

So who do we get to support us?

The people that make up your support system are going to be the people who care most about you. These people are usually family and friends (online and IRL) but can include people like teachers or neighbors. If you feel that you don't have anyone like that, there's a good chance that's the illness talking. It can be a little awkward but if you really think no one cares about you, ask them. Either they don't care about you and thus their opinion of you is irrelevant; or they do care about you and they'll be glad you came to them.

For some fucked up reason, direct communication isn't the standard practice in society. So some folks might shy away initially, but that awkwardness passes quickly. And It's important to get it out of the way as soon as possible. Because if these people are going to be the closest to you and help you get better—open and clear communication is gonna be par for the course. It's fine if it doesn't come easily at first, opening up about this stuff is hard, but keep at it.

Okay, so you found the people who are going to be your support system...so now what? Well this is where that whole concept of simplifying through outsourcing comes in. While the specific practices may change from person to person; the whole idea of a support system is to rely on them when there's something you can't do. The form of this that comes to mind for most people is emotional support. At least that's what I think of first when I hear the words "support system."

My mind conjures images of crying on the phone while a friend insists it will get better at two in the morning. Effectively outsourcing the handling of my emotions to someone else. This is a legitimate form of support and will probably be needed by all of us at some point or another. Although I do feel responsible to say that outsourcing your emotions in a crisis like that shouldn't be your go-to move. Ideally you want someone to help you shoulder the weight of your emotions and work through them. Just dumping them onto someone else isn't an effective form of long term support. But a true support system goes beyond just emotional support.

Uh, Maybe Don't?

You remember the spoons? It's time to bring those back because another form of support is tangible support. If you don't have the spoons to do a task or if doing a task will take all of your spoons; you can just ask someone else to do it for you. Obviously other people can't do things like eat for you, but they can wash the dishes or mail a letter. Simple daily tasks like that can feel crushing to some of us and prevent us from getting on with our other more important duties. But many other people don't mind doing those things—it doesn't cost them as many spoons. So if you have tasks like this in your life, discuss them with your support system and see what they can do.

Depending on the people that make up your support system and their own circumstances, they may not be able to just offer free labor. Even if they could, a lot of us would feel like a burden accepting it. The good news is that if you communicate openly you'll probably find what tasks have a high spoon cost for the people helping you. And while it isn't guaranteed, there's a chance that something hard for them is easy for you. If that happens you can work out how to trade tasks.

Let's say you struggle with laundry. You either don't have the time or don't have the energy to do it and knowing it needs to be done just eats away at the back of your brain. Meanwhile, you actually don't mind dusting or vacuuming. You just put on some music or a podcast and zone out while autopiloting your way through the tasks. It even feels good to see how clean things are when you're done. Well if you feel that way and you have a friend who doesn't mind laundry, just do a little switcheroo. They can pick up your laundry at the end of the week and while it's getting clean you can dust/vacuum their place. That way both of you avoid the task you hate the most but everything still gets done. That scenario is pretty idealized but you can usually find some form of it in your own life. Some people with ADHD will even have a friend call them and say they're coming over so that they will actually get up and clean their house. The friend doesn't always come over but thinking they will triggers something in our little ADHD minds that allows us to stop putting off a task and finally do it. That's a form of support that helps you and doesn't really require much from someone else.

A good support system will help you find a way to navigate life that works for you when the society proposed approach doesn't. And when it doesn't work out they'll be there to help you back on your feet. What that looks like is different for everyone, but anything that helps you get better is a valid approach. We're not meant to go through life alone. No matter how cool a loner looks or how loud our culture screams for independence.

If your life is a burden too heavy to bear on your own—ask for help. You'll probably be surprised how many people are willing to offer a hand and how much lighter that burden feels once they do. And even if you can't find a ton of people to pitch in; when it comes to support systems always go with quality over quantity. I may be able to count my support system on one hand but I know each one of them is someone I can count on. And they can count on me too which is the thing that helps the most sometimes. I've spent far too many nights feeling worthless. So when I get a call from a friend who needs me, it gives me a feeling of value. Here are two of my favorite quotes that talk about this:

> *"What you end up missing the most is the sweet burden of being needed. It gives your life a purpose. It really does. And it makes you feel great."*

> — Have Dreams Will Travel (2007)

Uh, Maybe Don't?

"And when nobody wakes you up in the morning, and when nobody waits for you at night, and when you can do whatever you want. What do you call it, freedom or loneliness?"

— Charles Bukowski

I've always said that I hate people but I like persons. I am a self proclaimed misanthrope after all. But we need other people, sometimes to help us and sometimes to be needed. So find your persons. Trust in them. And be someone they can trust in return.

Putting Yourself First
Life's A Movie And You're In Charge Of Casting

Life has often been compared to entertainment like movies and plays. I think this is because they're fun and exciting while also having a known structure. So much in our lives feels hectic and uncertain that we seek consistency wherever we can get it.

There's a trend amongst people with anxiety where we'll find ourselves rewatching the same TV shows over and over again. We'll usually call these our comfort shows even if the show itself isn't particularly happy (*cough* Supernatural *cough*). The comfort generally comes from the fact that we've seen the plot before and thus we can't be surprised by it. Our anxious minds know they can relax because they already know what's coming and don't have to be afraid of the unknown.

It's natural that we want the same thing from our lives. Sure, most of us don't want our lives to be stale and boring. But we also don't want to live our lives drowning in chaos. Viewing our life like a movie helps put the chaos around us into a familiar order. We usually identify ourselves as the main character and will assign the role of villain to whoever is pissing us off the most at the time. In recent years we've seen this role-based ideology become part of the standard cultural slang. It's common to open up social media and see someone talk about starting their Villain Era or Redemption Arc. A lot of folks even refer to periods in their life as seasons now. And I think it's because that structure makes more sense than the world around us usually does.

Humans have always tried to make sense of the world we live in; and learning all the things we've developed to do so is crazy. Here's one last sprinkling of poorly understood science. Did you know time isn't real? Like we literally made that shit up in order to make sense of our lives. This idea is still debated but let's explore it. Time at its most basic application is simply a unit of measurement for distance or entropy. Basically it's just a record of change. The idea of a second or minute or year is completely arbitrary; it's a measurement we assigned value, not one that originally had any. Like our planet went around a star and we all collectively lost our shit believing that mattered.

I don't bring this up to piss off the many folks smarter than me reading this, or to throw your very concept of reality into disarray. It's just to show that as far back as we can recall, humans have tried to make sense of the things that change around them. Whether it's the sun moving in the sky or just a friend we don't see anymore. Our minds crave understanding and structure. But don't worry, if you can't make your own, store bought is fine.

So we've established that life is a movie—let's work with that structure. It's clearly a favorite of mine, I got a whole-ass degree in it. You're the main character, the villain is a rotating role, and the genre changes week to week. Did I get that right? Well I don't fully agree with that division of roles. See, the main character isn't necessarily the protagonist. They're usually one in the same but not always. The difference is that the main character is the focus of the story but the protagonist is the character that drives the plot through their actions. So we don't want to just be the main character—we need to be the protagonist as well.

As enticing as it is, we can't allow ourselves to take a backseat in the story of our lives. I'm definitely guilty of doing this for a couple different reasons. First off I'm lazy as shit, facts are just facts. It is much easier to just focus on existing and allow everyone else around me to make any of the important decisions. After all humans are very adaptable so I'm sure that given enough time I can adjust to whatever the writers decide to put me through this season. And secondly, I didn't think I was allowed to be in charge. I spent my whole life growing up with all the adults around me saying I have to listen to them. Most things were decided for me and oftentimes whenever I tried to do something on my own I'd get yelled at. So when I entered the adult world and was suddenly in charge of everything, I didn't know what to do.

After being conditioned to not make any major decisions my whole life, my behavior adapted to that existence. To be clear I still had basic functions like feeding myself and taking a shower when I smelled. But choosing things like where to live, what to cook for dinner, or where to work? I was at a loss.

When I left home I didn't even know how to cook properly. Growing up we didn't really have money for spare food, so we couldn't afford the risk of me fucking up dinner. That fear is still deeply rooted in me to this day but luckily my partner has a mantra we live by *"We'll try it, and if it sucks we'll just get pizza."* Now even if the food turns out gross we usually eat it, we ain't got pizza every night money, but knowing I was allowed to try made a world of difference. And admittedly it took longer than it should have, but I realized this applied to most other things in my life as well.

For the better part of the last seven years I've existed in a state of spiraling paralysis. I didn't like how my life was going and it wasn't getting any better. But any thoughts to change it in a significant or meaningful way were either too scary to attempt or simply assumed to be off the table. Everything in my life felt locked in, including my mental illness.

I had gone to college and got a degree that I realized too late I couldn't use due to my mental illness and trauma. So I was stuck trying to find a job that would pay enough to cover my loan payments every month but didn't have any requirements for hire. I was stuck living in a state I hated because that's where my partner was and we couldn't afford to move. I was stuck with crippling undiagnosed gut health issues and a weak body. I was stuck being separated from all my friends. Stuck stuck stuck stuck stuck, I was so fucking stuck! But I wasn't.

The longer something has been established, the more ludicrous the idea of changing it becomes. But for better or worse we live with free will. If I wanted to right now I could get up, go buy a cake, and throw it at a random stranger on the street. Apart from breaking physics, there isn't much we can't do. There are however, many things that are difficult and/or rare to do. Like writing and publishing a book.

Sure I had always thought about it, I even started to write a couple times. But I wasn't someone who wrote books. The people who write books are smart and creative and have a good background and can concentrate for more than five minutes at a time. I wasn't like them, I was poor and clueless and had one good thought per decade. I wasn't allowed to write a book, that's not something someone like me does. That's what I thought. That was how I thought about everything in my life. Like I was stuck in place unable to stop the falling dominos just out of reach. Doomed to see them complete the only path available.

But I was wrong. The things I hated in my life didn't need to stay that way, I was allowed to change them. There is literally nothing that says I can't get up today and just start writing a book, exercising, or getting my health in check. I might feel silly at first trying to change something unmovable in my mind. It may take some time and results might be slow but progress is progress. To lose weight at a healthy rate is only 1-2 pounds a week. To write this book I just spent one uninterrupted hour each day working on it until it was done. It didn't matter how much I got done in a single day, what mattered was that I stuck with a goal I set for myself. I finally had something to be proud of and I really needed that. I think we all need something to be proud of.

The version of myself I saw in my head wasn't a predestined fact. I got so hung up on my mental self image that when I wanted to do something new I'd compare it to that image. And when they didn't match I thought that new thing was off the table. Looking back I feel so dumb over this. I was literally discriminating against myself. Whether it was because of a societal view I internalized or just my deep rooted mental illness; I still can't say. But if you've felt this way, like you're not allowed to do something just because of who you've been, I gotta tell ya—you're wrong bud.

You can always change your path in life if you don't like the one you're on. Sure money can be quite the hurdle to get over, but it's doable. Everyday you get to make the choice whether you're gonna just be the main character or if you're gonna be the protagonist. And the more often you pick to be the protagonist, the more control over your movie you're gonna have. Pick the protagonist enough and you can even change your genre. It took a few months but consistent small choices let me change this shit from a tragedy to a comedy. Even if the news keeps trying to make it horror/science fiction. Here's a quote I love that kind of summarizes everything:

> *"It takes a long time to realize how truly miserable you are, and even longer to see that it doesn't have to be that way."*
>
> — Bojack Horseman (Season 3, Episode 3)

With this metaphor firmly established, let's get to the point of this chapter's title. Casting is one of the most important parts of any project. Unfortunately the casting of our lives often feels out of our hands. When you go to school or work you can only encounter the other people who already go there. Your options for interactions are inherently limited. The place this affects us most is when it comes to our families. Family is one of those things we often feel we can't escape from; it's so bad I could say *"you can pick your friends but you…"* and anyone on Earth could finish the sentence.

The idea that family is a permanent decision that you weren't allowed to make, is massively ingrained into the core of our culture. There're endless sayings I could quote here but I do want to try and have some original thoughts in this book. What most sayings boil down to is that you get the family you get and despite how dogshit they might be, you can't leave them. I would like to take this moment to say with my full chest that that's a load of shit. Sure you can't control the family you're born into. But you have every right to leave them if you want to. To be clear I mean leaving as in going to a new town, not the other kind of leaving this book is about.

I lead into this with family and will focus on that pretty heavily; but know that what I talk about can be applied to friends, romantic partners, or anyone in your life.

Just as we can find people who care about us and can help us immensely as a support system, the opposite is also true. You can meet people that are just the worst. I'm sure we all know someone who we fucking hate, but I'm not talking about them. When I say you can meet people who are the worst, I mean for you—personally. The common term these days is toxic, a person so shitty they poison you by proxy.

So what am I supposed to do about them?

Dealing with a toxic person is usually pretty hard to do. The people who are blatantly garbage don't normally make it into the inner parts of our lives. So by the time we notice someone is toxic they're usually already attached to one or more parts of our lives. It can be hard to even notice how toxic someone is if they've been in your life long enough. If they've been there for a very long time (like since birth) you may feel that cutting them out of your life isn't even an option. Or that if it is an option it may not be worth the pain and complications of doing so. But you control the casting of your life.

I recommend you to take an inventory of the things in your life that affect how you feel. Review all the nouns; all the people, places, and things. This should take awhile, don't rush it. Once you have all these things listed out, I want you to really think about how they make you feel the majority of the time.

If while doing this you find people that are toxic in your life, who make you feel bad or get you to do things you regret; start to think about how to remove them. These can be people you've shared good memories with, are related to, or even love. But if when you're honest with yourself, you know they cause harm in your life; they are most likely toxic and need to be separated from you. At least while you heal. They'll probably be mad and feel hurt but you need to put yourself and your healing first. It sounds harsh but you can't get better if you're constantly being poisoned.

Sometimes the toxic thing in our lives isn't the people around us but the places we go and live in. If you've ever listened to pop punk or emo music you've definitely heard some version of the line *"I hate this town and I can't wait to leave."* It might sound childish but the places we live have a strong effect on us.

I grew up in a place known for being violent, dirty, and broke. One of the nicknames for it was literally *"The Dirty D."* It had a reputation of being trashy and over time the people felt they were destined to live up to that reputation. Many of the people I knew growing up who never left our hometown ultimately became the kind of people they hated and complained about. This isn't just limited to my shitty hometown, I've heard from friends all over the country that it happens in their hometowns too.

Places can be just as toxic as people if not moreso. As humans we want so badly to be accepted into the group because of our dumb monkey brain. Given enough time we'll slowly change into the people around us just so we don't feel alone. So if you notice that you're living in a place that affects you negatively, please don't be afraid to leave.

Even if you like where you are, please move out of your hometown at some point in your life. This isn't directly connected to mental health but it's definitely important to living a full well rounded life. The world is massive and has so many diverse things to offer. New sights, new people, new points of view. If you hate being alive, this will help show you that you've only experienced one version of it and there are more to choose from. Moving out of your hometown or especially your state will teach you more than you can anticipate. If afterwards you find you liked your hometown best then you can move back; but open yourself to new takes on life.

<u>What if I'm scared?</u>

Then you're human. Leaving home and feeling like you have to start from scratch is so fucking terrifying—but at the same time it's very liberating. It might be hard but given time and good planning you can move to a better place, a happier place. I hated living in my hometown, I never felt comfortable there. But when it came time to leave for college I found myself constantly crying. Leaving everything I knew and going somewhere where I knew no one and had no built in support scared the shit out of me. Plus I was mourning the loss of the friends I had made back home who I finally felt truly close to. Like I felt as though I had JUST gotten my shit together and figured things out, only to have to leave.

It took some time but eventually I knew that the move was for the best. For one of the first times in my life I was surrounded by people who had no preconceived idea of me. I could put forth the best parts of myself, try finding new ones, and leave some of my baggage behind. I ended up making some good friends, having some heartbreak, and learning a lot about myself and the world. It's a shame that adventure came with a six figure price tag. One I'll be paying back until I'm dead, but oh well.

One of the things I noticed after moving was how much I loved having a beautiful place to walk around safely and sing. I couldn't take casual walks back home—I'd get shot. And even though I'm not a fan of being in nature (I don't fuck with bugs), I learned that being near nature helped calm my mind. Unfortunately since I graduated, I settled in an area with no nature and I don't feel comfortable going anywhere. So I've sat at home and rotted away waiting to leave. Where you live matters, don't be afraid to try and find the right place for you.

The loss of cutting out a part of your life is initially going to hurt. Whether it's a person, an activity, or an entire place; it can be complicated and confusing trying to fill the spaces left behind. So before you make any major decisions; I would recommend that you get advice from someone you trust who knows your situation. I can offer endless general advice but your life is unique and will require a unique set of solutions. But once you've put yourself first, done the work, and cut out the toxic parts of your life— you'll be surprised how fast you heal.

I spent most of my life thinking that certain fundamental things just weren't on the table when it came to changing my life. I thought I was stuck with my shitty family, in my shitty town, with my shitty life path. Since I was about seven years old I would swear up and down that I'd be dead by twenty five. It was literally impossible for me to see the fundamental parts of my life changing in any positive way. So when my twenty fifth birthday came and went I was at a bit of a loss. The version of life that I was so certain was unchangeable had changed. It made me start to wonder what other things I had overlooked.

Growing up I was convinced my parents hated me. In my younger years I would constantly get in trouble at school for anger problems or being uncooperative. On one occasion I had gotten in trouble at school a few times in a week for asking too many questions and not listening to my teachers instructions. While driving me home from a meeting with my teacher, my mom and I had this exchange.

Mom: *"Why are you like this? What's wrong with you?"*
Me: *"This is just who I am."*
Mom: *"THEN. BE. SOMEONE. ELSE!"*

I don't think I need to explain how having that said to you could fuck up a nine year old kid. That comment has lived in my mind my entire life and it was one of the things I'd point to as evidence that my Mom didn't love me and wanted a different kid. But I was wrong on both counts.

While I don't want to suggest that any or all parental abuse is simply misguided love, because it's not; parents are just other humans. As I grew up and gained experiences of my own, I could start to see what my parents' life was actually like. As well as the abilities they either did or did not have available to deal with it. They had difficulties and stressful days and they didn't have the answers to everything. Sometimes they'd fuck up and say something they didn't mean out of frustration. Just like I fuck up, so do they from time to time, we're all human and we're all fallible. Your parents are literally just two people who boned one time. There is no reason to believe that made them perfect caretakers. And yeah, some of them are literally the fucking worst, no arguments there. But in most of the parental relationships I've seen; parents usually do love their kids, they just suck at communicating.

Honestly if you start paying attention to people, you'll notice pretty quickly that like 70% of them can't communicate for shit. And maybe it's just the autism in me, but I find direct communication to be the best in the long run. Too often people act as if everyone knows what they're thinking or feeling, as if it's a given. Some folks treat indirect communication as a test to see if the listener really cares. Sometimes it just feels too awkward to speak our feelings out loud so people don't. But if you're under the belief that no one around you cares about you, ask them. It will be awkward for a minute; but that's better than isolating yourself due to your assumptions of what other people feel.

This whole section of the book has been about putting yourself first and doing what's best for you. Cutting out toxic parts of your life and trying new things. Whatever changes you need to make in order to feel better, you should strive for them regardless of how others feel. I think this is a crucial part of making a life you'll like enough to want to live. But it's equally crucial to not go too far in this approach.

So am I supposed to cut people out or forgive them?

At the cost of sounding like a broken record, you need a balanced approach to most things in life. Putting yourself first is incredibly important and will probably involve cutting some people out of your life. But if you go scorched earth to do so, you might find there's little left to enjoy once you're better. The grass can't be greener if it's gone. I know it sounds contradictory, but cutting everyone who isn't perfect out of your life and moving away isn't going to solve your problems. In most cases it's just going to leave you feeling alone and wondering what the point of getting better even was if you have no one to share it with. So while you go through this process, just try not to be an asshole about it. Have some empathy and realize that everyone you see is just another person trying to figure this life shit out.

There's actually a word for this feeling or thought process. It's called "Sonder"; the realization that every random passerby is living a life as rich and vivid as your own.

Everyone has their own hopes and dreams, ups and downs, and strengths and weaknesses. There exist entire histories of worlds within each of us. That guy who cut you off in traffic was once five years old at the park and scraped his knee. He cried so hard he couldn't talk as his grandma put a bandaid on it and gave it a kiss. She hugged and shushed him to peace until he forgot the pain and all he remembered was how she smelled of lilacs. That's a first person memory for him and he's got a million more like it.

Everyone you interact with or see out in the world has their own life going on. For most of us managing that one life is a full time task. It's rare for someone to have enough spare mental bandwidth to consider someone else's life and feelings. It's important to remember this when you find yourself upset with how someone handled something or even the world at large. Not everyone was mean or failed you on purpose, sometimes they just failed. Failed to communicate a thought or feeling, failed to remember something important, or failed to act the way they wanted to. And if we're going to accept that it's okay for us to fail sometimes, then we need to accept that of others too.

So put yourself first but do it with empathy. Don't become the villain of someone else's story just to change your own. If you find you need to change the cast of your life to become the protagonist, then so be it. You can recast or cut their part entirely, that power belongs to you. Just make sure that when you're done, you're left with a movie you're proud of and want to share.

Be kind to yourself and to others.

You're Gonna Be Okay
I'm Proud Of You

So we're at the last chapter. It wasn't a very long book but I hope it was potent in its content. I'm sure at this point you have a pretty good image of me in your head and I hope that by showing my flaws and being honest I've made you feel a little less alone. Honestly if you've read this whole book you probably know more about me than most of the people I've known in my life. To me that makes us friends and I hope you feel the same.

My goal when starting this book was to help others while helping myself. I make no effort to try and cover up the fact that I'm broke and trying to make money off of this. I'm honestly at the end of my rope and have been getting by on borrowed time and the kindness of others for a while now. So I really need something to turn my life around and offer direction on what path to pursue in the future. I can only hope that this book has been a worthwhile purchase for you.

My thinking when making a book on such a serious subject in such a nonchalant way, was that people like me would respond best to advice if it came from a friend like them. If I could cut through the veil of professionalism and just talk to you like a regular person, I thought that'd be the best way to connect. On some level I think I was trying my best to be my version of Sean from Good Will Hunting. Feel free to let me know if my non-conventional approach was the one that finally worked for you.

Endings are never easy. You always wonder if you've made your point well, wrapped up all your thoughts, and presented your ideas clearly. I know for me even a good ending leaves me unsatisfied and wanting more. I'm never quite ready to say goodbye to something that's meant a lot to me. But endings are inevitable and we can always carry the emotions and lessons we've learned with us well past the credits.

You've learned so much in this short span of time. You had the courage to pick up this weird little book. You learned how to appreciate your good days and to have your bad ones. You got the help you needed from those who care about you and learned how to accept it. You took the brave step of finding out what the control room in your head needs and how to get it. You put yourself first with grace and empathy, showing the value you place on your life. And you found a myriad of reasons to stay both big and small.

You have done so much and I know it wasn't easy—it certainly wasn't for me. But you stuck with it, you gave it your all no matter how long it took, and you're still here. That's an amazing accomplishment and it continues to be every day you stay. Your effort was meaningful and thanks to that effort and your courage, you're gonna be okay.

I hope you had a laugh or two along the way (I like to think I'm funny) and enjoyed some of my media recommendations and references. If everything felt a little disjointed please forgive me; I've never written a book before. But I have one last little janky set of recommendations for you as you grow past these pages.

Uh, Maybe Don't?

As silly as it sounds, two of the things that influenced me moving forward the most were the game series Dark Souls and the anime Mushoku Tensei. If you're unfamiliar I'll fill you in on them.

Dark Souls is a video game series known for being hard and punishing, but the game is *usually* fair. While playing you'll experience the process of failing over and over again but getting a little better each time until you finally succeed. That feeling and knowing that sometimes progress isn't always happening visibly but instead internally; that would motivate me in hard times. It was a safe way to learn an important lesson so I recommend you give it a try if you're into video games. Just be kind to yourself and know you're supposed to fail, it's how you learn.

The other thing I mentioned, Mushoku Tensei, is an anime based on a novel of the same name. The story follows someone who suffered serious trauma as a kid and could never get past it, becoming a shut in. With no friends or positive influences they were isolated in their room and essentially raised by the internet. This caused their morals and world view to get pretty fucked up. After certain events lead to them being kicked out on the street; they end up dying while trying to save someone. They then awake as an infant born into a new world with magic and other cool fantasy stuff. Realizing they now have a second chance at life, they do their best not to waste it this time. They pour time and effort into bettering themselves physically and the people around them help to better them mentally and emotionally.

Watching someone overcome their traumas and change slowly over time to become a better person is so captivating to me. The main character doesn't start as a good person and this puts a lot of people off. But getting to see a realistic depiction of someone seemingly past saving become better is very motivating. The story follows his full life and develops an extremely rich world along the way. This isn't the tale of one event or journey that changed someone, this is watching someone slowly change and get better over the course of a lifetime. There are setbacks and the main character fucks up and regresses at times, like we all do. But eventually they keep moving forward. I love this series and would recommend it wholeheartedly, especially if you think you're irredeemable or incapable of change.

One of the lines from the opening song of the show's second season has continued to motivate me and I hope it does the same for you.

> *"With just a little bit more courage, there was a tomorrow that could have changed. I didn't even realize that, how many times did I have those moments?"*

> — Spiral by LONGMAN

I find that sometimes a message can be said a hundred different ways but only one of them will stick. For me this line was what finally stuck. I knew that if I put in effort things would change eventually but it felt too hard to do that. The very word effort itself is intimidating for me. So when I heard this line and instead of effort it talked of courage, that worked for me. That idea that if I just have a little bit of courage today, then there will be a tomorrow I can change.

For whatever reason that plays in my head when I don't want to work on something or just want to give up. I don't need to do a lot, I don't need to complete something right now; I just need a little bit of courage to start the process.

It might sound silly but that line and that show have honestly changed my life in a positive way. It became a mantra for me when trying to write this book. A cheat code to defeat the inertia of my mind. I hope one of the quotes I've used or even one of my own lines can have a similar impact for you in your life.

So there it is, my final recommendation and borrowed lesson. I hope that if you watch anything I suggested, you'll save me a seat in your mind, and see why it meant so much to me.

Just because this book is over doesn't mean you're gonna be on your own again. You can start from the beginning whenever you want or skip to a favorite line. The me in this book isn't going anywhere and I'll always be here when you need me—even if my lines get a little stale after a while.

But I hope that in the future, a long time from now, my home is on a dusty forgotten shelf in the corner of your life. To me that's the best ending of all. The one where you don't need me anymore.

I'm so very proud of you.

Your friend,
Jesse

Special Thanks

I never would have wrote this book or made it this far in life if it wasn't for several special people. If me or this book has meant something to you, please take a moment to join me in acknowledging the people who have meant the world to me.

First, forever and always, is my Partner. She loved me when I didn't think I could ever be loved, and showed me that I was something that could be lost. Her support has meant more than any arrangement of words could express. And if this book has helped anyone it is because she helped me first. She also listened to all of my rants, a herculean labor I am very thankful for.

Thank you to my family. While we've had our rocky moments, recent years have shown your care for me when I needed it most. When I was a week away from killing myself cause I ran out of money and couldn't land a job, my mom noticed despite me being states away. She scraped up what little money she had and came up with all the excuses she could to give it to me in a way I could accept, that saved me. Three months later when I finally got a job interview but had literally no money and couldn't pay my insurance in order to legally drive to it, my sibling sent me what I needed, no hesitation. And once my father knew I wanted to try writing he consistently encouraged me to go for it, he even gave me the money to copyright this book. Thanks to all of you.

Thank you to my friend and editor K. When it comes to grammar and professional writing I was so out of my depth but she had me covered. Despite not speaking for several years due to life keeping us too busy, she was immediately delighted to offer her help. Catching up over this book has been wonderful. True friends never fade.

Thank you to all of the friends who tried to support me in any of the endeavors I tried before this one. While those endeavors didn't work out, your support meant the world to me.

Thanks to anyone who has ever talked with me through the night long enough to see the sunrise. Serious conversations or goofy ones. In a bathroom or on a walk. Sober or not. Those moments made me feel much less alone and gave me good memories to look back on for a lifetime.

And lastly, thank you Hunter. You were a wonderful friend who really helped to boost my opinion of myself. Lord Of The Rings marathons, making terrible movies, and the best vacation I ever had; you left me with some amazing memories. You are very missed everyday by everyone who knew you. But hey, I did it, I kept my promise. I'm still here.